The Moonlit Stream

and other poems

Compiled by

John Foster

OXFORD
UNIVERSITY PRESS

OXFORD
UNIVERSITY PRESS

Great Clarendon Street, Oxford OX2 6DP

Oxford University Press is a department of the University of Oxford.
It furthers the University's objective of excellence in research, scholarship,
and education by publishing worldwide in

Oxford New York
Athens Auckland Bangkok Bogotá Buenos Aires Calcutta
Cape Town Chennai Dar es Salaam Delhi Florence Hong Kong Istanbul
Karachi Kuala Lumpur Madrid Melbourne Mexico City Mumbai
Nairobi Paris São Paulo Shanghai Singapore Taipei Tokyo Toronto Warsaw

and associated companies in Berlin Ibadan

Oxford is a trade mark of Oxford University Press
in the UK and in certain other countries

© Oxford University Press 2000
First published 2000

British Library Cataloguing in Publication Data
Data available

ISBN 0 19 917364 8

Printed in Hong Kong

The National Literacy Strategy termly requirements for poetry at Year 6 are fulfilled on the following pages:

Term 1

pp 7, 11, 20, 27, 33, 34, 38.

Term 2

pp 6, 8, 10, 14, 16, 18, 19, 22, 23–26, 28, 30, 32, 35–36, 41–42, 49–52, 54, 57–61, 64, 66–67, 69, 70, 72, 75–76, 83–85, 88, 89, 90.

Term 3

pp 12, 19, 46, 47, 68, 77–78, 80, 86.

For more detailed information on the poetry range requirements and the termly objectives, see Oxford Literacy Web Poetry Teacher's Guide 2.

Contents

A Poem

A poem springs
From simple things

A random thought
By fancy caught

A silver note
From a redbird's throat;

A sighing breeze
From lofty trees;

A pale young moon
That fades too soon;

A tender time
Of some lost dream

A bird's swift flight
A starlit night;

The tender bliss
Of a farewell kiss;

A tiny hand
That gently clings –

From these small things
A poem springs.

Geraldine M Johnson

The Splendour Falls on Castle Walls

The splendour falls on castle walls
    And snowy summits old in story:
The long light shakes across the lakes,
    And the wild cataract leaps in glory.
Blow, bugle, blow, set the wild echoes flying,
Blow, bugle; answer, echoes dying, dying, dying.

O hark, O hear! How thin and clear,
    And thinner, clearer, farther going!
O sweet and far from cliff and scar
    The horns of Elfland faintly blowing!
Blow, let us hear the purple glens replying:
Blow, bugle; answer, echoes, dying, dying, dying.

O love, they die in yon rich sky,
    They faint on hill or field or river:
Our echoes roll from soul to soul,
    And grow for ever and ever.
Blow, bugle, blow, set the wild echoes flying,
And answer, echoes, answer, dying, dying, dying.

Alfred, Lord Tennyson

The Moonlit Stream

A stream far off beneath the moon
    Flowed silver-bright and thin,
Winding its way like some slow tune
    Played on a violin.

The valley trees were hushed and still;
    The sky was pearly grey;
The moonlight slept upon the hill –
    As white as snow it lay.

Then softly from a ruined tower
    That rose beside the stream
A bell chimed out the midnight hour;
    And then – Oh, did I dream? –

Then all at once a long, black boat
    With neither sail nor oars
Down that bright stream began to float
    Between its shadowy shores.

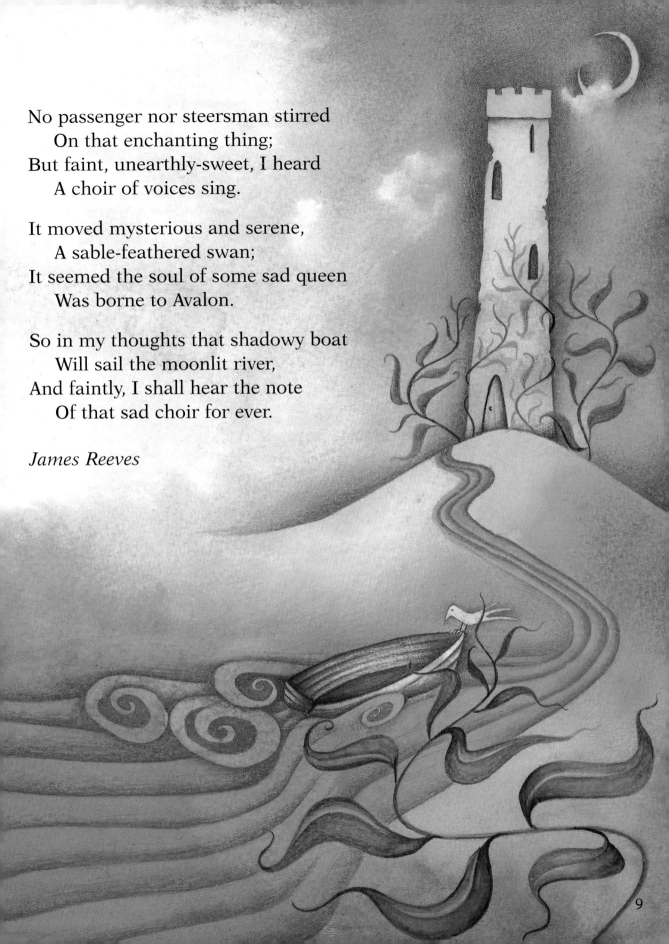

No passenger nor steersman stirred
    On that enchanting thing;
But faint, unearthly-sweet, I heard
    A choir of voices sing.

It moved mysterious and serene,
    A sable-feathered swan;
It seemed the soul of some sad queen
    Was borne to Avalon.

So in my thoughts that shadowy boat
    Will sail the moonlit river,
And faintly, I shall hear the note
    Of that sad choir for ever.

James Reeves

My Unicorn

My Unicorn
How Beautiful
In Dew of Dawn
My Unicorn
Washes his Horn
In the Forest Pool
My Unicorn
How Beautiful.

John Whitworth

Westward! Westward!

From **The Song of Hiawatha**

On the shore stood Hiawatha,
Turned and waved his hand at parting;
On the clear and luminous water
Launched his birch-canoe for sailing,
From the pebbles of the margin
Shoved it forth into the water;
Whispered to it, 'Westward! westward!'
And with speed it darted forward.
　　And the evening sun descending
Set the clouds on fire with redness,
Burned the broad sky, like a prairie,
Left upon the level water
One long track and trail of splendour,
Down whose stream, as down a river,
Westward, westward Hiawatha
Sailed into the fiery sunset,
Sailed into the purple vapours,
Sailed into the dusk of evening.

H W Longfellow

Six Views of a Waterfall

When the river threw itself off the cliff
It spun a twist of rope
So as not to lose touch with itself.

The river of a sudden
Tired of lying down between fields
And having the sky painted on its face
Stood up and was pleased.

Around the holy water where the miracle happened
They hollowed out a damp chapel
And glued green carpets on the wall to absorb the sound.
Every day someone brings fresh ferns.

We can see the silent film through the beaded curtain
There is interference on the vertical hold
And for a comedy there should be subtitles,
But the actors shout just the same.

Sometimes the river stays still
And children swim upstream.
After a time they lie down and walk away.

At home they have sardines for tea
And later go to bed.
While this is going on
The waterfall does what it has always done
And doesn't dream about people.

Gareth Owen

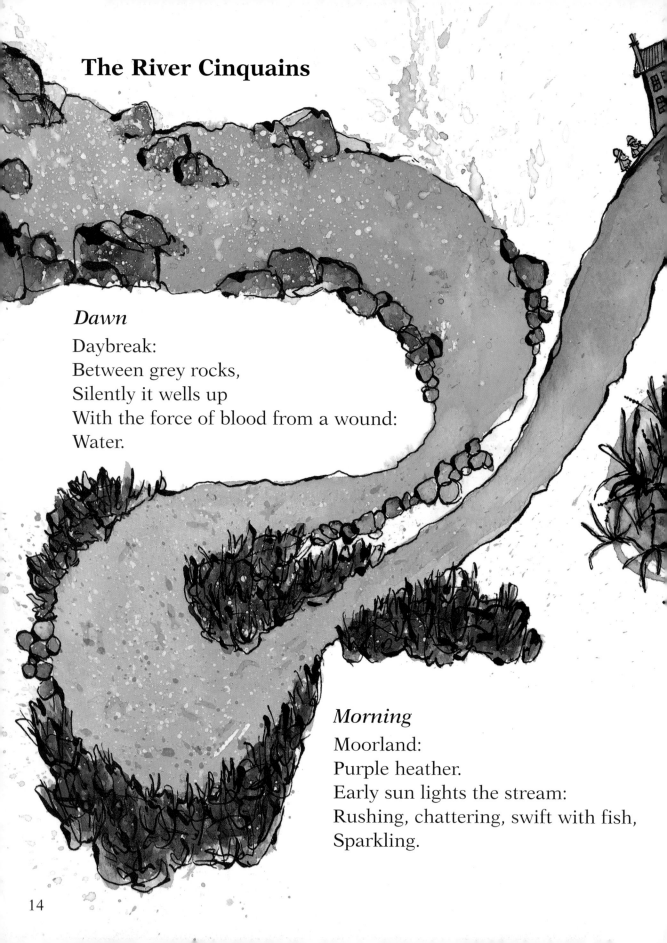

The River Cinquains

Dawn

Daybreak:
Between grey rocks,
Silently it wells up
With the force of blood from a wound:
Water.

Morning

Moorland:
Purple heather.
Early sun lights the stream:
Rushing, chattering, swift with fish,
Sparkling.

Afternoon

Townscape:
Water reflects
Grey brickwork, dull windows.
Fishermen stare. The river moves
Slowly.

Evening

Salt-marsh:
Under lead skies
The water slides away.
From the damp banks of sand a few
Birds call.

Night

Moon shines
On open sea:
The swell gleams with silver
And on a distant shore the first
Waves break.

Nigel Cox

Daughter of the Sea

bog seeper
moss creeper
growing restless   getting steeper

trickle husher
swish and rusher
stone leaper   splash and gusher

foam flicker
mirror slicker
pebble pusher   boulder kicker

still pool
don't be fooled
shadow tricker   keeping cool

leap lunger
crash plunger
free fall   with thunder under

garbage binner
dump it in her
never mind her   dog's dinner

plastic bagger
old lagger
oil skinner   wharf nagger

cargo porter
weary water
tide dragger   long lost daughter

of the sea
the sea the sea
has caught her   up in its arms and set her free

Philip Gross

The Beach

The beach is a quarter of golden fruit,
a soft ripe melon
sliced to a thick green rind
of jungle growth;
and the sea devours it
with its sharp white teeth.

William Hart-Smith

The Seashell's Prayer

I am whispering.
Are you listening?
Father Neptune,
Hear my plea.

I need you to rock me,
Soothe me,
Set the music
In me free.

Come and save me,
Father Neptune.
I am homesick
For the sea.

Sue Cowling

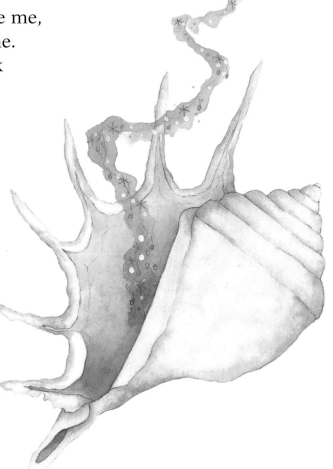

From **The Rime of the Ancient Mariner**

With sloping masts and dipping prow,
As who pursued with yell and blow,
Still treads the shadow of his foe,
And forward bends his head,
The ship drove fast, loud roared the blast,
And southward aye we fled.

And now there came both mist and snow,
And it grew wondrous cold:
And ice, mast-high, came floating by,
As green as emerald.

And through the drifts the snowy clifts
Did send a dismal sheen:
Nor shapes of men nor beasts we ken -
The ice was all between.

The ice was here, the ice was there,
The ice was all around:
It cracked and growled, and roared and howled,
Like noises in a swound!

Samuel Taylor Coleridge

Tree Song

City of whispers,
symphony of sighs,
intricate embroidery
sampling the skies.

Machinery of nature,
factory of air,
delirious dancer
dishevelling her hair.

Tony Mitton

Wild Flower

Our uncut lawn to me alone brings joy,
With shaggy dandelion suns, grass bound;
To me they are not weeds, do not annoy,
Each ragged clump of leaves with light seems crowned.
I cannot understand my father's haste
To weekend mow and sever every head;
Though pleasing him, it leaves a barren waste,
A bare expanse of green, where once was spread
An emerald carpet buttoned down with gold.
So it looks now, with here and there a cloud
Of softest grey as tawny heads grow old.
Unseen I pluck each clock and laugh aloud.
I know, of course, they do not tell the hour,
But breath-blown seeds will fall, take root … and flower!

Catherine Benson

Two Tanka

Lost in the blue sky,
a fluttering dot warbles,
pours out, liquid sound.
It vanishes beyond sight,
but notes still cascade like rain.

Bright dandelions;
golden suns in a green sky,
quite soon, translated
into cloud like globes above
an undulating green sea.

Marian Swinger

Four Haiku

Cut out of silver,
the star next to the moon's face
hangs like an ear ring.

Open the window …
a smell of rain arises
closer than friendship.

Leopards are fearful,
but, at the sniff of danger
burn like a fireball.

Silver coated moon
hurrying through the dark sky
won't you wait for me?

Jean Kenward

Earth Riddles

Painted glass bauble,
swung on an unseen thread.

Curled palette of light,
splashed on dark canvas.

Lapis lazuli,
brush-stroked with white.

Lone marble,
rolled over threadbare velvet.

A medal,
pinned to the blue blazer of night.

Space-hopper,
cast like a kite over silent seas.

Small change
in a deep pocket.

Judith Nicholls

An Emerald is as Green as Grass

An emerald is as green as grass;
    A ruby red as blood;
A sapphire shines as blue as heaven;
    A flint lies in the mud.

A diamond is a brilliant stone,
    To catch the world's desire;
An opal holds a fiery spark;
    But a flint holds fire.

Christina Rossetti

For Forest

Forest could keep secrets
Forest could keep secrets

Forest tune in everyday
To watersound and birdsound
Forest letting her hair down
to the teeming creeping of her forest-ground

but Forest don't broadcast her business
No, Forest cover her business down
from sky and fast-eye sun
and when night come
and darkness wrap her like a gown
Forest is a bad dream woman

Forest dreaming about mountain
and when earth was young
Forest dreaming of the caress of gold
Forest rootsing with mysterious Eldorado

And when howler monkey
wake her up with howl
Forest just stretch and stir
to a new day of sound

but coming back to secrets
Forest could keep secrets
Forest could keep secrets

And we must keep Forest.

Grace Nichols

29

A Tomcat Is

Nightwatchman of corners
Caretaker of naps
Leg-wrestler of pillows
Depresser of laps

A master at whining
And dining on mouse
Afraid of the shadows
That hide in the house

The bird-watching bandit
On needle-point claws
The chief of detectives
On marshmallow paws

A crafty yarn-spinner
A stringer high-strung
A buttermilk moustache
A sandpaper tongue

The dude in the allcy
The duke on the couch
Affectionate fellow
Occasional grouch

J Patrick Lewis

The Prayer of the Cat

Lord,
I am the cat,
It is not, exactly, that I have something to ask of You!
No –
I ask nothing of anyone –
but,
if You have by some chance, in some celestial barn,
a little white mouse,
or a saucer of milk,
I know someone who would relish them.
Wouldn't You like some day
to put a curse on the whole race of dogs?
If so I should say,

AMEN

Carmen Bernos de Gasztold
(translated by Rumer Godden)

The Owl

When cats run home and light is come,
And dew is cold upon the ground,
And the far-off stream is dumb,
And the whirring sail goes round,
And the whirring sail goes round;
Alone and warming his five wits,
The white owl in the belfry sits.

When merry milkmaids click the latch,
And rarely smells the new-mown hay,
And the cock hath sung beneath the thatch
Twice or thrice his roundelay,
Twice or thrice his roundelay;
Alone and warming his five wits,
The white owl in the belfry sits

Alfred, Lord Tennyson

Weathers

This is the weather the cuckoo likes
    And so do I;
When showers betumble the chestnut spikes,
    And nestlings fly:
And the little brown nightingale bills his best,
And they sit outside at 'The Travellers' Rest',
And maids come forth sprig-muslin drest,
And citizens dream of the south and west
    And so do I.

This is the weather the shepherd shuns,
    And so do I;
When beeches drip in browns and duns,
    And thresh, and ply;
And hill-hid tides throb, throe on throe,
And meadow rivulets overflow,
And drops on gate-bars hang in a row,
And rooks in families homeward go,
    And so do I.

Thomas Hardy

November

November is a grey road
Cloaked in mist.
A twist of wood-smoke
In the gathering gloom.
A scurrying squirrel
Hoarding acorns.
A steel-grey river
Glinting in the twilight.
A grey rope
Knotted around a threadbare tree.

John Foster

The Frozen Man

Out at the edge of town
where black trees

crack their fingers
in the icy wind

and hedges freeze
on their shadows

and the breath of cattle,
still as boulders,

hangs in rags
under the rolling moon,

a man is walking
alone:

on the coal-black road
his cold

feet

ring

and

ring.

Here in a snug house
at the heart of town

the fire is burning
red and yellow and gold:

you can hear the warmth
like a sleeping cat

breathe softly
in every room.

When the frozen man
comes to the door,

let him in,

let him in,

let him in.

Kit Wright

A Smuggler's Song

If you wake at midnight, and hear a horse's feet,
Don't go drawing back the blind, or looking in the street.
Them that asks no questions isn't told a lie.
Watch the wall, my darling, while the Gentlemen go by!
    Five and twenty ponies,
    Trotting through the dark –
    Brandy for the Parson,
    'Baccy for the Clerk;
    Laces for a lady, letters for a spy,
And watch the wall, my darling, while the Gentlemen go by!

Running round the woodlump if you chance to find
Little barrels, roped and tarred, all full of brandy-wine,
Don't you shout to come and look, nor use 'em for your play.
Put the brushwood back again – and they'll be gone next day!

If you see a stable-door setting open wide;
If you see a tired horse lying down inside;
If your mother mends a coat cut about and tore;
If the lining's wet and warm – don't you ask no more!

If you meet King George's men, dressed in blue and red,
You be careful what you say, and mindful what is said.
If they call you "pretty maid", and chuck you 'neath the chin,
Don't you tell where no one is, nor yet where no one's been!

Knocks and footsteps round the house – whistles after dark –
You've no call for running out till the house-dogs bark.
Trusty's here, and *Pincher's* here, and see how dumb they lie –
They don't fret to follow when the Gentlemen go by!

If you do as you've been told, 'likely there's a chance,
You'll be given a dainty doll, all the way from France,
With a cap of Valenciennes, and a velvet hood –
A present from the Gentlemen, along o' being good!
    Five and twenty ponies,
    Trotting through the dark –
    Brandy for the Parson,
    'Baccy for the Clerk.
Them that asks no questions isn't told a lie –
Watch the wall, my darling, while the Gentlemen go by!

Rudyard Kipling

The Flower-fed Buffaloes

The flower-fed buffaloes of the spring
In the days of long ago,
Ranged where the locomotives sing
And the prairie flowers lie low:
The tossing, blooming perfumed grass
Is swept away by the wheat,
Wheels and wheels and wheels spin by
In the spring that still is sweet.
But the flower-fed buffaloes of the spring
Left us, long ago.
They gore no more, they bellow no more,
They trundle around the hills no more:
With the Blackfeet, lying low,
With the Pawnees, lying low,
Lying low.

Vachel Lindsay

Alabama

My brethren,
among the legends of my people
it is told how a chief,
leading the remnant of his people,
crossed a great river,
and striking his tipi-stake upon the
ground,
exclaimed, "A-la-ba-ma!"
This in our language means
"Here we may rest!"
But he saw not the future.
The white man came:
he and his people could not rest there;
they were driven out,
and in a dark swamp
they were thrust down into the slime
and killed.
The word he so sadly spoke
has given a name to one of the white
man's states.
There is no spot under those stars
that now smile upon us,
where the Indian can plant his foot
and sigh "A-la-ba-ma."

Khe-Tha-A-Hi (Eagle Wing)

For Sale:

Eliza Keturah MacDonald,
age twelve years

Offered: one hale
and hearty lass
who is good at cooking
gives no sass
is slow to bed
and swift to rise
who never puts
her tongue to lies.

Strong as an ox
she'll plough and hoe.
A willing one,
she won't say no
to any service
you request.

Be sure that she
will do her best
and justify the
fifty pound
we ask for her
in the next round
of auctions.

Given at Kingston Town
by hand of Jonas Helwig Brown
this twenty-seventh of July
eighteen eleven, anno domini.

Pamela Mordecai

Mama Dot

Born on a sunday
in the kingdom of Ashante

Sold on monday
into slavery

Ran away on tuesday
cause she born free

Lost a foot on wednesday
when they catch she

Worked all thursday
till her head grey

Dropped on friday
where they burned she

Freed on saturday
in a new century

Fred D'Aguiar

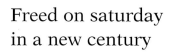

The Last Tiger

Soon there will be no more of us;
I am the last of all my tribe.
Here I wait, O my father,
My fangs rotten to stumps and black blood
Amongst the clapboard hovels of the suburbs.
Here I wait, O my sons who never were
In the days of my dying,
The gunshot festering in my hollow side,
Filling my belly on the wind.
Here I wait, O my ancestors,
Amongst the tin cans and the dustbins,
Gnawing at my broken paw,
The kingdom of my spirit
Shrunk to a white-hot tip of hate.
Here I wait, O my cousins,
To kill this old woman
Who will limp across the cinders
With two buckets in her hands.

But I have a dream, O my gods,
I have a dream
That shuts out the hunger and the dying;
I have a dream,
That in my ancient, burning strength
I will roam the ancient cities of mankind
And, screaming, claw the stolen coats
Of you, my honoured sisters and brothers
From the backs of rich and beauteous ladies.
Thus, do not ask me why I hate women.

Gareth Owen

A Message
from a Long Serving Member
of the Brown Party

Vote for me
Your friendly earthworm,
Conservationist
Born and bred.
When I take your soil
I'll always give
Something better back instead.
I'm into things organic
And really most concerned
That you cast your vote
To ensure
The earthworm
Is returned.

Pat Moon

Dear Mrs Spider

The Ancient Order of Insects
Beetle Drive
Antrim

Dear Mrs Spider,

Your application form has come to my attention
but it raises issues that I need to mention.
Apparently you have eight legs
Which is two too many
And when asked to fill in "Type of wings"
You declared that you hadn't any.
You say your body is in only two parts
when the required number is three;
You call your home a web
and like to eat flies for tea.

Therefore, I am afraid that I must reject
Your request to become AN INSECT.

Yours

The Chief Bluebottle
(Membership Secretary)

John Coldwell

Advertisement

Are your children peaky and thin?
Too many late nights? Too much telly?
Forest air and a fattening diet
    Will very soon put things right!

A week or two at Sweetmeat Cottage
Is bound to make them scrumptiously chubby.
Children just love my gingerbread house,
    My liquorice doors and chimney.

There's everything here to delight a child,
And one kind lady to see to their needs –
For I love children, tasty little darlings!
    Apply without delay!

C J D Doyle

Scylla's Black Diary

Dear Diary,
I'm fed up.
We've had some awful weather,
And I'm up to here with sailors,
Twelve today – tough as old leather.

If you ask me
They'd rowed straight here
From Circe's, she's a great one
For changing people, mmm, I'm sure
There was a hint of bacon.

That's Charybdis burping,
Downstairs,
Gulps her water, never sips.
Now she's under doctor's orders,
Simple diet, fish and ships.

And old Zeus is throwing tantrums –
Shocking night with all this rain –
There he goes, a bolt of lightning
Missed Odysseus
… again.

Does my heads in all that wailing
Don't those sirens ever sleep?
Time for beddie-byes dear Diary,
Off to brush six sets of teeth.

Petonelle Archer

53

Christmas Thank Yous

Dear Auntie
Oh, what a nice jumper
I've always adored powder blue
and fancy you thinking of
orange and pink
for the stripes
how clever of you

Dear Uncle
The soap is
terrific
So
useful
and such a kind thought and
how did you guess that
I'd just used the last of
the soap that last Christmas brought

54

Dear Gran
Many thanks for the hankies
Now I really can't wait for the flu
and the daisies embroidered
in red round the 'M'
for Michael
how
thoughtful of you

Dear Cousin
What socks!
and the same sort you wear
so you must be
the last word in style
and I'm certain you're right that the
luminous green
will make me stand out a mile

Dear Sister
I quite understand your concern
it's a risk sending jam in the post
But I think I've pulled out
all the big bits
of glass
so it won't taste too sharp
spread on toast

Dear Grandad
Don't fret
I'm delighted
So *don't* think your gift will
offend
I'm not at all hurt
that you gave up this year
and just sent me
a fiver
to spend

Mick Gowar

Reindeer Report

Chimneys: colder.
Flightpaths: busier.
Driver: Christmas (F)
Still baffled by postcodes.

Children: more
And stay up later.
Presents: heavier.
Pay: frozen.

Mission in spite
Of all this
Accomplished.

MERRY CHRISTMAS

U A Fanthorpe

Parrot Fashion

There was a school teacher from York,
Who taught her young parrot to talk;
He recited his tables
And all Aesop's fables,
And then took a bow, with a squawk.

Coral Rumble

7X7

Once upon a time...

Brave Brownie

A Brownie I know called Rebecca
Was a bold and adventurous trekker
But though brave as could be
She would not climb a tree
'Cos she thought a woodpecker would peck her.

Michael Day

Lim

There once was a bard of Hong Kong,
Who thought limericks were too long.

Gerard Benson

Accidental Proverbs

It takes two to flog a dead horse.
Still waters come but once a year.
Rats run deep.
When in doubt, desert a sinking ship.
Revenge wasn't built in a day.
A contented mind must be endured.
Don't cut off your nose in mid-stream.
Gather ye rosebuds where credit is due.
Curiosity is mightier than the sword.
Seeing is blind.
Ignorance killed the cat.
Absence is the best sauce.
Love is the mother of invention.
Necessity springs eternal.
Travel broadens the mouth.
Look before you grow fonder.

Robert Hull

Questions and Answers

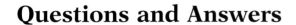

Q: What's inside the sun?

A: Daytime.

Q: What's inside the earth?

A: Colours before they get their names.

Q: Who made the first circle?

A: Someone who got very dizzy.

Q: What draws the bee to the honeysuckle?

A: Ten million summers.

Q: What roars inside a seashell?

A: Beach lions.

Q: What roars inside of you?

A: My blood.

Q: How does one tie a rainbow?

A: The first thing is to find the ends.

Q: If it's noon here, what time is it on Mars?

A: A billion years before noon.

Q: How long does it take to move a mountain?

A: Depends on the number of ants available.

Q: At what speed does a moth move to a lamp?

A: At light speed.

Q: Why is the letter "i" dotted?

A: To have a good time.

Zaro Weil

WordPerfect

In the stinking dark hole
in the middle of the wild woods
the fox received a fax.

In the outbacks of Australia
near the aboriginal's river
the emu got an e-mail.

In the middle of the Atlantic ocean
in the cold mid-winter,
the fish went on the Net.

In the wooden shanty house
in the shanty town
the spider got on the Web.

In the highlands of Scotland
by the tall Scots pine trees
the ram loaded ram.

Scuttling across the desert
in the desperate heat,
the mouse clicked the mouse.

Running across the prairies
for the first time,
the floppy foal got a file.

In the smelly stinky barn of a small dairy farm,
the hen wrote with a quill pen,
the secret of the universe.

Jackie Kay

Spoonerisms

Though it fell from the fourth floor
I'm pleased to say
The cat popped on its drawers
And walked away.

I've toiled and sweated for many an hour;
I'm stopping now to shake a tower.
Then I'll have a cocoa in a mug
And fight a liar and be real snug.

The teacher complains while
The pupil sits and squirms:
"You have hissed my mystery lessons
And tasted two worms!"

Eric Finney

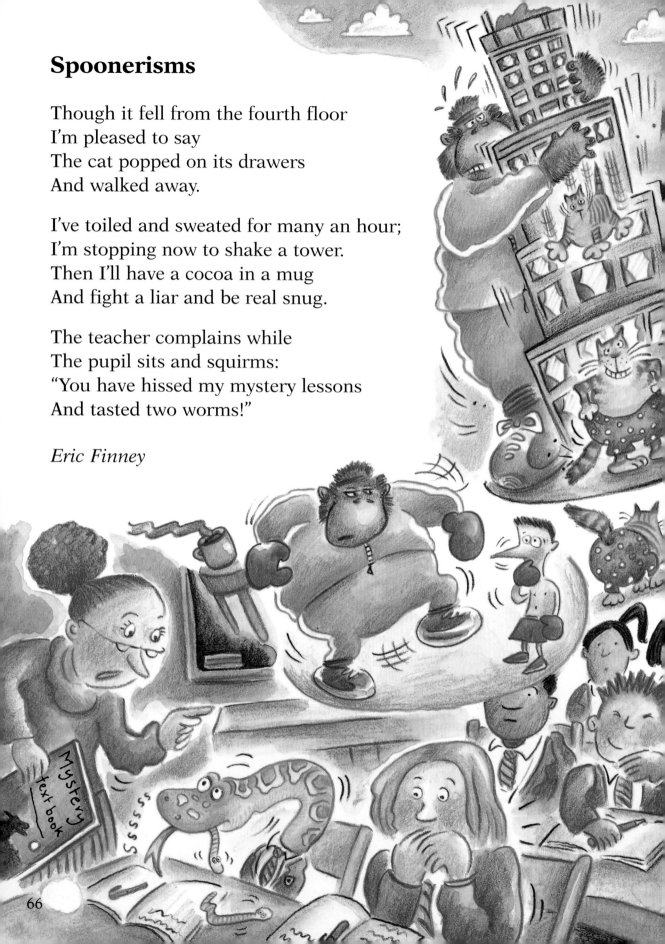

A Cross Stick?

A cross stick?
Can't understand what sir's
Rabitting
On about.
So
Thought
I'd
Compose a poem instead.

John Foster

Private? No!

Punctuation can make a difference.

> Private
> No swimming
> Allowed

does not mean the same as

> Private?
> No. Swimming
> Allowed.

Willard R Espy

An Attempt at Unrhymed Verse

People tell you all the time,
Poems do not have to rhyme.
It's often better if they don't
And I'm determined this one won't.
                              Oh dear.

Never mind, I'll start again.
Busy, busy with my pen … cil
I can do it if I try –
Easy, peasy, pudding and gherkins.

Writing verse is so much fun,
Cheering as the summer weather,
Makes you feel alert and bright,
'Specially when you get it more or less the
                    way you want it.

Wendy Cope

Writing a Sonnet

"Today we're going to write in sonnet form,"
My teacher said. I wondered what she meant.
Apparently we all had to conform
To some set pattern, but my mind was bent
On playing noughts and crosses with my friend.
"AB, AB, CD, CD, EF,
EF, GG" I did not comprehend,
And to the word "pentameter" was deaf.
She spoke of iambs, and I do recall
"So all day long the noise of battle roll'd,"
Though what to do with this wherewithal
In fourteen lines, was like a tale untold.

I've got the rhythm, but the words won't come.
Tee tum, tee tum, tee tum, tee tum, tee tum.

Pam Gidney

Write-a-Rap Rap

Hey, everybody, let's write a rap.
First there's a rhythm you'll need to clap.
Keep that rhythm and stay in time,
'cause a rap needs a rhythm and a good strong rhyme.

The rhyme keeps coming in the very same place
so don't fall behind and try not to race.
The rhythm keeps the rap on a regular beat
and the rhyme helps to wrap your rap up neat.

'But what'll we write?' I hear you shout.
There ain't no rules for what a rap's about.
You can rap about a robber, you can rap about a king,
you can rap about a chewed up piece of string ......
(well you can rap about almost ...... anything!)

You can rap about the ceiling, you can rap about the floor,
you can rap about the window, write a rap on the door.
You can rap about things that are mean or pleasant
you can rap about wrapping up a Christmas present.

You can rap about a mystery hidden in a box,
you can rap about a pair of smelly old socks.
You can rap about something that's over and gone,
you can rap about something going on and on and on
      and on ......

But when you think there just ain't nothing left to say ......
You can wrap it all up and put it away,
It's a rap. It's a rap. It's a rap rap rap rap RAP!

Tony Mitton

Out in the City

When you're out in the city
Shuffling down the street,
A bouncy city rhythm
Starts to boogie in your feet.

It jumps off the pavement
There's a snare drum in your brain,
It pumps through your heart
Like a diesel train.

There's Harry on the corner
Sings, 'How she goin' boy?'
To loose and easy Winston
With his brother Leroy.

Shout, 'Hello!' to Billy Brisket
With his tripes and cow heels,
Blood-stained rabbits
And trays of live eels.

Maltese Tony
Smoking in the shade
Keeping one good eye
On the amusement arcade.

And everybody's talking:

Move along
Step this way
Here's a bargain
What you say?
Mind your backs
Here's your stop
More fares?
Room on top.

Neon lights and take-aways
Gangs of girls and boys
Football crowds and market stalls
Taxi cabs and noise.

From the city cafes
On the smoky breeze
Smells of Indian cooking
Greek and Cantonese.

Well, some people like suburban life
Some people like the sea,
Others like the countryside
But it's the city
Yes it's the city
It's the city life
For me.

Gareth Owen

Change Our Ways

I own an orchard
But I won't give you one apple.

I cultivate a beanfield.
I sell you soya at good profit.

I have an education.
I use it to put one over on you.

My shelves are full of books.
I won't teach you to read.

I glory in bright silks to wear.
I give you cast-offs.

I have much to learn.
Will you teach me?

Angela Topping

Just One Day

Mum lost her job and couldn't pay
the rent
so they took our home away.

From a flat
        to the street
took just one day.
Now people rush past
and look away
they think only animals
live this way.

So spare some change or just some time –
Homelessness is not a crime.
I'm a person – my name is Caroline.

Lindsay Macrae

Song of the Refugee Child

I may be little but let me sing,
I may be a child but let me in.
What does it matter if I read or write?
You'll send me to war to learn to fight.

I am the refugee child.

I am the hungry of a hundred lands,
mine is the blood that stains the white sands,
but I'll climb your barbed wire and walls of stone
and find a free place to make a new home.

I am the refugee child.

I am the dispossessed, wandering one,
you can't kill me with your bomb and your gun.
I am the face that looks out from the night
towards your rich window with its warmth and its light.

I am the refugee child.

I am a child of the family called Poor
and I am coming to knock on your door.
I may be little but let me sing,
I may be a child but you must let me in.

I am the refugee child.

Robin Mellor

On Television Tonight

And now the desert runs
in leaps and bounds
over the plains

and overtakes the ox
who's famished
and slow

and has too may ribs
and nowhere to go.

The ox is slow and sinks to its knees.

The river got tired long ago.

The desert with its hungry stride
gains ground
on people
who've forgotten
where green has gone.

Tonight the desert wins.

On millions of screens
we follow the losers
trailing nowhere
in never-ending columns
so many mothers
whose breasts are empty rivers
so many children
with arms as thin as a whisper.

Then the ad breaks in to say
look at the scrumptious goo
queuing up for you,
have a nice day
look the other way.

But we've just seen
a different screen

and heard it scream.

Robert Hull

79

A Change of Scene

I couldn't stay, I couldn't go.
What was it there that held me so
Between the darkness and the light?
Two ghosts who would not leave my sight.

They seemed a mother and her child
Picnicking in a golden field
And not a cloud was in the sky
And nobody was asking why.

I couldn't sleep, I couldn't wake.
It felt as if a storm might break
But not on them, not there, oh no
Not on that scene which held me so

Until it changed, when suddenly
Those ghosts took one last look at me,
The field grew dark, the golden land
Was nothing but a waste of sand.

Nothing but dust stretched on and on,
The mother and her child had gone
And in their place no picnicking
But hunger vaguely wandering.

Millions of mothers crouching there,
Millions of children eating air.
I couldn't go, I had to stay.
It's only dreams that go away

And this was not a dream, I knew.
The day had come, the night was through
And everyone was asking why,
And so was I. And so was I.

John Mole

Hunger

This is hunger. An animal
all fangs and eyes.
It cannot be distracted or deceived.
It is not satisfied with one meal.
It is not content
with a lunch or dinner.
Always threatens blood.
Roars like a lion, squeezes like a boa,
thinks like a person.

The specimen before you
was captured in India (*outskirts of Bombay*),
but it exists in a more or less savage state
in many other places.

Please stand back.

Nicholas Guillen

The Paint Box

I had a paint box –
Each colour growing with delight;
I had a paint box with colours
Warm and cool and bright.
I had no red for wounds and blood,
I had no black for an orphaned child,
I had no white for the face of the dead,
I had no yellow for burning sands.
I had orange for joy and life,
I had green for buds and blooms,
I had blue for clear bright skies.
I had pink for dreams and rest
I sat down and painted Peace.

Tali Shurek, aged 13
Be'er Shera, Israel

The Tree and the Pool

'I don't want my leaves to drop,' said the tree.
'I don't want to freeze,' said the pool.
'I don't want to smile,' said the sombre man,
'Or ever to cry,' said the Fool.

'I don't want to open,' said the bud,
'I don't want to end,' said the night.
'I don't want to rise,' said the neap-tide,
'Or ever to fall,' said the kite.

They wished and they murmured and whispered,
They said that to change was a crime,
Then a voice from nowhere answered,
'You must do what I say,' said Time.

Brian Patten

Somewhere in the Sky

Somewhere
In the sky,
There's a door painted blue,
With a big brass knocker seven feet high.
If you can find it,
Knock, and go through –
That is, if you dare.
You'll see behind it
The secrets of the universe piled on a chair
Like a tangle of wool.
A voice will say,
'You have seven centuries in which to unwind it.
But whatever
You do,
You must never,
Ever,
Lose your temper and pull.'

Leo Aylen

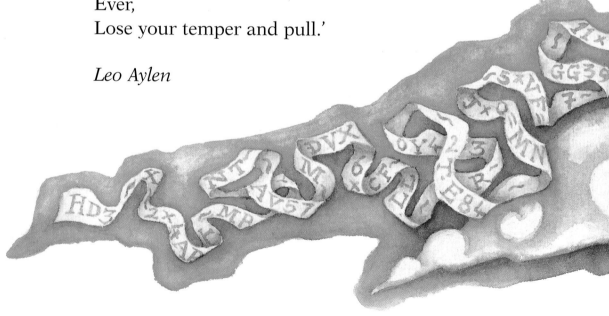

86

There Will Come Soft Rains

There will come soft rains and the smell of the ground,
And swallows calling with their shimmering sound;

And frogs in the pools singing at night,
And wild-plum trees in tremulous white;

Robins will wear their feathery fire
Whistling their whims on a low fence-wire;

And not one will know of the war, not one
Will care at last when it is done.

Not one would mind, neither bird nor tree,
If mankind perished utterly;

And Spring herself, when she woke at dawn,
Would scarcely know that we were gone.

Sara Teasdale

Dreams

Hold fast to dreams
For if dreams die
Life is a broken-winged bird
That cannot fly.

Hold fast to dreams
For when dreams go
Life is a barren field
Frozen with snow.

Langston Hughes

Hope

Hope is a climber,
A brimming cup,
The elevator that only
Goes up,
A chair lift
Over the drop,
Swinging you to the
Mountain top...
Hope is the stretch
You make to reach
The branch that holds
The perfect peach.
Hope is a bird
Learning to fly,
Wobbling after
Many a try
Then taking off
to the giddy high,
Windy blue silk
Summer sky...
Hope is the moment
When you jump
Up from the tumble,
Out of the slump.
Hope is the light in the awful dark,
The clear, bright-blazing, beckoning spark
That sets your feet to a running pace
For one little look at her beautiful face.

Mary O'Neill

Index of First Lines

Acknowledgements

The editor and publisher are grateful for permission to include the following poems:

Petonelle Archer: 'Scylla's Black Diary', copyright © Petonelle Archer 2000, first published in this collection by permission of the author; **Leo Aylen:** 'Somewhere in the Sky' from *Rhymoceros: Poems by Leo Aylen* (Macmillan, 1989), republished in *Somewhere in the Sky* (Nelson, 1996), reprinted by permission of the author; **Catherine Benson:** 'Wild Flower', copyright © Catherine Benson 1993, first published in *Earthways Earthwise* (OUP, 1993), reprinted by permission of the author; **Gerard Benson:** 'Lim' from *Does W Trouble You?* (Viking, 1994), reprinted by permission of the author; **John Coldwell:** 'Dear Mrs Spider', copyright © John Coldwell 2000, first published in this collection by permission of the author. **Wendy Cope:** 'An Attempt at Unrhymed Verse', reprinted by permission of the author; **Sue Cowling:** 'The Sea-Shell's Prayer' first published in *Sandwich Poets 4* (Macmillan, 2000), reprinted by permission of the author; **Nigel Cox:** 'The River Cinquains', copyright © Nigel Cox 1986, first published in *Poetry 2* by John Foster (Macmillan Publishers, 1986), reprinted by permission of the author; **Fred D'Aguiar:** 'Mama Dot' from *Mama Dot* (Chatto & Windus), reprinted by permission of The Random House Group Ltd; **Michael Day:** 'Brave Brownie', copyright © Michael Day 2000, first published in this collection by permission of the author; **Carmen Bernos De Gaztold:** 'The Prayer of the Cat' from *Prayers from the Ark* by Carmen Bernos de Gaztold translated by Rumer Godden (1963), reprinted by permission of the publisher Macmillan Children's Books. **Cornelius Doyle:** 'Advertisement', copyright © Cornelius Doyle 2000, first published in this collection by permission of Gerard Benson;
Willard R Espy: 'Private? No!' from *The Best of the Almanacs of Words at Play*; **U.A Fanthorpe:** 'Reindeer Report' from *Standing To* by U.A. Fanthorpe, (Peterloo Poets, 1982), reprinted by permission of the publisher;
Eric Finney: 'Spoonerisms', copyright © Eric Finney 2000, first published in this collection by permission of the author; **John Foster:** 'November', copyright © John Foster 1995, reprinted from *Standing on the Sidelines* (OUP, 1995); 'A Cross Stick', copyright © John Foster 2000, first published in this collection, both by permission of the author; **Pam Gidney:** 'Writing a Sonnet', copyright © Pam Gidney 2000, first published in this collection by permission of the author; **Mick Gower:** 'Christmas Thank Yous' from *Swings and Roundabouts* (HarperCollins Publishers), reprinted by permission of the author; **Philip Gross:** 'Daughter of the Sea' from *The All-Nite Café* (Faber and Faber Ltd), reprinted by permission of the publisher. **Nicholas Guillen:** 'Hunger' from *The Great Zoo* edited by Robert Marquez (Monthly Review Press, 1972), reprinted by permission of the publisher;
Langston Hughes: 'Dreams' from *The Dream Keeper and Other Poems* by Langston Hughes (Alfred A Knopf, Inc), copyright © Alfred A Knopf 1932, renewed 1960 by Langston Hughes, reprinted by permission of David Higham Associates Ltd; **Robert Hull:** 'Accidental Proverbs' and 'On Television Tonight', both copyright © Robert Hull

2000, first published in this collection by permission of the author; **Jackie Kay:** 'Wordperfect' from *The Frog Who Dreamed She Was an Opera Singer* by Jackie Kay (Bloomsbury, 1998), reprinted by permission of the publisher; **Jean Kenward:** 'Four Haiku', copyright © Jean Kenward 2000, first published in this collection by permission of the author; **Rudyard Kipling:** 'A Smuggler's Song' from *Rudyard Kiplings Verse, The Definitive Edition* (Hodder & Stoughton, 1945), reprinted by permission of A P Watt Ltd, on behalf of The National Trust for Places of Historic Interest or National Beauty. **Patrick J Lewis:** 'A Tomcat Is', copyright © Patrick J Lewis, first published in this collection by permission of the author; **Vachel Lindsay:** 'The Flower-Fed Buffaloes' from *Going to the Stars* (Hawthorn Books), copyright 1926 by D Appleton & Co, renewed 1954 by Elizabeth C Lindsay, reprinted by permission of Dutton Children's Books, a division of Penguin Putnam Inc. **Lindsay Macrae:** 'Just One Day' from *You Canny Shove Yer Granny Off a Bus* (Viking, 1995), copyright © Lindsay Macrae 1995, reprinted by permission of Penguin Books Ltd. **Robin Mellor:** 'Song of the Refugee Child', copyright © Robin Mellor 2000, first published in this collection by permission of the author. **Tony Mitton:** 'Tree Song' from *Plum* (Scholastic Children's Books, 1998), copyright © Tony Mitton 1998, reprinted by permission of David Higham Associates Ltd; 'Write-A-Rap Rap', copyright © Tony Mitton 2000, first published in this collection by permission of the author. **John Mole:** 'A Change of Scene', copyright © John Mole 1992, from *The Conjuror's Rabbit* (Blackie, 1992), reprinted by permission of the author. **Pat Moon:** 'A Message from a Long Serving Member of the Brown Party' from *Earthlines* (Pimlico, 1991), copyright © Pat Moon 1991, reprinted by permission of the author. **Pamela Mordecai:** 'For Sale', copyright © Pamela Mordecai 2000, first published in this collection by permission of the author. **Judith Nicholls:** 'Earth Riddles', copyright © Judith Nicholls 2000, first published in this collection by permission of the author. **Grace Nichols:** 'For Forest' from *Come On Into My Tropical Garden* (A & C Black Publishers Ltd, 1988), copyright © Grace Nichols 1988, reprinted by permission of Curtis Brown Ltd, London, on behalf of Grace Nichols. **Mary O'Neill:** 'Hope' from *Words, Words, Words*, copyright © Mary O'Neill 1966, © renewed Erin Baroni and Abigail Hagler 1994, reprinted by permission of Marian Reiner. **Gareth Owen:** 'Out in the City', 'Six Views of a Waterfall' and 'The Last Tiger' from *Selected Poems* (Macmillan, 2000), reprinted by permission of the author. **Brian Patten:** 'The Tree and the Pool' from *Gargling With Jelly* by Brian Patten (Viking, 1985), copyright © Brian Patten, 1985, reprinted by permission of Penguin Books Ltd. **James Reeves:** 'The Moonlit Stream' from *Complete Poems for Children* (Heinemann), reprinted by permission of Laura Cecil Literary Agency, on behalf of the James Reeves Estate. **Coral Rumble:** 'Parrot Fashion' first published in *Creatures, Teachers and Family Features* by Coral Rumble (Macdonald Young Books, 1999), copyright © Coral Rumble 1999, reprinted by permission of the author. **Marian Swinger:** 'Two Tanka', copyright © Marian Swinger 2000, first published in this collection by permission of the author. **Sara Teasdale:** 'There Will Come Soft Rains' from *The Collected Poems of Sara Teasdale* (Macmillan Publishing Company, 1937), copyright Macmillan Publishing Company 1937, copyright © renewed by Morgan Guaranty Trust Company of New York 1965, reprinted by permission of Scribner, a division of Simon & Schuster. **Angela Topping:** 'Change Our Ways' copyright © Angela Topping 2000, first published in this collection by permission of the author. **Zaro Weil:** 'Questions and Answers' from *Mud, Moon and Me* first published in the UK by Orchard Books, 1989, a division of The Watts Publishing Group Ltd, 96 Leonard Street, London, EC2A 4XD, reprinted by permission of the publisher. **John Whitworth:** 'My Unicorn' from *The Complete Poetical Works of Phoebe Flood* (Hodder & Stoughton Ltd), reprinted by permission of the publisher. **Kit Wright:** 'The Frozen Man' from *Rabbiting On* (Collins, 1978), reprinted by permission of the author.

Although we have tried to trace and contact holders before publication, in some cases this has not been possible. If contacted we will be pleased to rectify any errors or omissions at the earliest opportunity.

The Artists

Stephen Gulbis p 11;

Alan Hayball pp 49, 50;

George Hollingworth pp 60, 68–69;

Steve Hutton pp 20–21, 52–53;

Rhian Nest James c/o Kathy Jakeman p 46;

Christina Kilby p 75;

Mary McQuillan pp 26–27;

Diana Mayo pp 18–19;

Anna Menzies pp 14–15;

Chris Molan pp 38–40;

Chay Nicholson p 41;

Lindy Norton pp 61–63;

Rebecca O'Reilly pp 32, 35;

Rachel Pearce pp 42–43, 78–79, 80–82;

Julia Pearson pp 47–48;

Louise Rawlings pp 33, 90–91;

Petra Rohr Rouendaal pp 44–45;

Clare St Louis Little p 77;

Evie Safarewicz c/o John Hodgeson pp 28–29;

Eric Smith pp 22–23;

Jamie Smith c/o Peters Fraser & Dunlop pp 70–71;

Mary Claire Smith pp 76, 84–85;

Annabel Spenceley c/o J Martin & Artists p 57;

Martin Ursell c/o Kathy Jakeman p 7;

Sarah Warburton c/o Sylvie Poggio pp 72–74;

Suzanne Watts pp 24–25, 34;

Stephen Waterhouse pp 64–65;

Doffy Weir pp 54–56;

Lisa Williams c/o Sylvie Poggio pp 58–59;

Lucy Wilkinson pp 88–89;

Alison Dexter Wong pp 12–13;

Hilary Yaniw p 51